Implementing Enterprise Data Warehousing

A Guide for Executives

Alan Schlukbier

Raleigh, North Carolina, USA
www.schlukbier.com

ISBN: 978-1-4303-1063-1

Printed in the United States of America.

Difficult things take a long time, impossible things a little longer.

To Jean, Jill, Paula, & Andrew and special thanks to Glenn, the greatest fisherman I've ever known.

Forward

"'Cheshire Puss,' she began, rather timidly...' Would you tell me, please, which way I ought to go from here?' 'That depends a good deal on where you want to get to, 'said the Cat. 'I don't much care where—'said Alice. 'Then it doesn't matter which way you go,' said the Cat." Alice's Adventure in Wonderland, by Lewis Carroll.

So many books have been written on the subject of software development. The problem is that I can remember only a very few that have been really helpful in rationalizing an existing diverse environment with the new de Jour technology or technique I was trying to implement.

Very few businesses have the luxury to start from a clean slate and just ignore all prior technologies. Consequently, the average large enterprise is inundated with a diverse set of technologies which often adds to the confusion rather than the organization. The problem, however, is usually not the technology but rather how to implement the new technology or technique in a real, breathing, working organization of people.

I also object to the average length of these books which are simply too long to ever read in their entirety. I have, therefore, determined to write a small book, a précis really that presumes an existing diverse technology base in a large enterprise. The emphasis is in knowing how to implement loosely-connected relational data structures in a creative yet structured way that can be successful in any culture.

Too often, management is oversold on either the benefits of business information or data warehousing tools without being told the whole program that is necessary for utilizing these new approaches. This book is dedicated to explaining a complete program that I have found necessary to really be successful in implementing enterprise data warehousing and business information analytics that serves the entire enterprise.

Preface

It has been some time now that I have wanted to produce a small précis or primer that outlines the steps necessary for a co-ordinated effort to build a better organization and plan for enterprise-level data warehousing and business information analytics. Initially, I thought that Executives could use this book to make sure they were on track or to remind them of the steps, but lately I realize that all sorts of people and skill levels have to be marching at the same drum beat.

The problem is that in technology and often business, people tend to isolate themselves and view the world only through their particular perspective. It is hard to get everyone to view the enterprise in which they are working as a whole. Some people object to this saying, "how can you view something so large with so many products, services, and different types of customers to serve on one page?" The point is that if we can't, then we cannot hope to all retain the same enterprise image in our minds. Nor can we agree on the best tactical plan to employ in reshaping or changing the enterprise to meet new business requirements.

When we cannot or will not make these changes we cannot expect our analytical tools to help us. The organization often becomes defensive and inflexible or not willing to invest the time and effort in training to take advantage of these tools.

Acknowledgements

There are so many men and women I want to acknowledge that have helped me during 15 years of often tumultuous consulting assignments. Two people especially stand out. Both were former bosses who provided countless hours of counseling and more backroom support than I will ever know. Doug Jensen was the first to give me a job in Canada and his leadership in Gulf Canada as the IT department went through some very difficult transitions was truly inspiring.

Tom Meaders was my next boss who really provided the consistent logic necessary to keep a staff together that was constantly being asked to do the impossible. Tom's communications ability and fine analytic acumen provided much needed support as we designed and implemented over 8 conformed Kimball Data-Marts. None of this could have been done without him.

I would also like to acknowledge John Tench who was the President of my local DAMA Chapter at IRMAC (Information Resource Management Association of Canada) and subsequently provided me with two very interesting consulting assignments. He remains the most knowledgeable Data Warehousing expert in Toronto.

There were others such as Lawrence Watson, compatriot from Gulf Canada who has continually encouraged me in my career as it moved from Toronto, to Winnipeg, to North Carolina. Such friends are once in a lifetime. Larry has the finest intellect I have ever known and the forgiving nature of a true friend.

I cannot leave this section without acknowledging my good friend from Winnipeg, Gino Braha, who has provided tireless Executive consulting there for over 30 years. Also, Erik Lindquist and all my friends in *Tiger Trends Consulting* who encouraged me to remain true to objective methodology and a love for *Tim Horton's* donuts. Last but by no means least, is to thank my brother, George, for his unfailing support and excellent Sunday dinners.

Contents

1	Need for Architecture...............................	1
2	Why This Book Is Important.........................	3
3	Phases...	7
4	Phase I – Information.................................	10
5	Phase I – Deliverables...............................	18
	A. Data Quality Program............................	18
	B. Data Stewardship Program........................	19
	C. Central Data Model...............................	20
	D. Data Governance..................................	22
6	Phase II – Implementation...........................	30
7	Phase II – Deliverables..............................	39
	A. ETL Program......................................	39
	B. Backup / Recovery................................	41
	C. Archive / Purging................................	42
8	Phase III – BI, Data Mining, and Review............	50
9	Phase III – Deliverables.............................	58
	A. BI Architecture..................................	58
	B. Data Mining......................................	61
	C. Master Data Management............................	64
	D. SOA Architecture.................................	65
	E. Enterprise Information & Integration..............	66
	F. Portals, Collaboration, & Other Content Sharing..	67
	G. Review and Future Trends.........................	69
10	Closing Remarks......................................	73
	Glossary...	77
	Bibliography..	93
	About the Author....................................	97

1

NEED FOR ARCHITECTURE

1962 was the year that Dr. Ed Codd first proposed an architecture and plan that promised to revolutionize the information world. It was the birth of the relational data base (some organizations today are still struggling with maintaining 3rd Normal Form data bases).

Dr. Ed recognized early on the problem was with trying to maintain redundant copies of the same data across several data stores. All had to remain in sync and were both difficult and expensive to maintain. His idea was to eliminate redundant data and to make all data accessible from the same data source. His design was such a simple solution and also solved the performance problem as well. Today, we are beginning to extend that same design to redundant services or processes that need to be rationalized and maintained in one location (SOA – Service-Oriented Architecture). These ideas have had and will continue to have a profound affect on organizations of all sizes but particularly those enterprises large enough to have several lines of business or services which may also offer a considerable amount of complexity in interfacing with a multitude of shareable resources of data stores and services.

IMPLEMENTING ENTERPRISE DATA WAREHOUSING
A GUIDE FOR EXECUTIVES

We need a better blueprint! Better architecture and better models are our only hope to illustrate and coordinate all the many levels of complexity in building a living breathing information enterprise that will not collapse under its own weight. There simply must be a logical communication device that illustrates the complexity for all to see for both businessman and technologist. We must also provide a methodology to constantly rationalize and reorganize our structure in a safe, incremental step by step non-destructive manner. This methodology should allow us to provide products and services even as we update and extend those same products and services.

Again, we must stand on the shoulders of giants and acknowledge our debt to relational data structures and the modern application of modeling techniques. There is simply no other way and those who try and fail do so because they have not covered all the fundamentals and convinced their clients of the logic of the argument.

The solution to complexity is better architecture which, in turn, calls for better modeling which is certain to lead to better communication and understanding and more rationalizing into simpler more powerful designs.

It only takes space. This is our only resource which can resolve all complexity with logical data structures.

2

WHY THIS BOOK IS IMPORTANT

"If you can't describe what you are doing as a process, you don't know what you're doing!" William Edwards Deming, distinguished American economist, 1931.

Since the early 60's there has been quite a plethora of software tools all designed to make software programming easier, faster, and more maintainable (reliable). The only methodology to survive these tools that speaks to the large enterprise needs is *Model-Driven Development*. Tools will come and go just as the languages used to describe processes, but methodology must remain stable.

It is easy to teach a programmer some arcane language and it is even easier to allow him to produce system after system of legacy (unmaintainable) code that even his colleagues cannot make heads or tails. But to produce code that is consistent, maintainable, and reliable requires examination and testing by a variety of people. These people are not only involved in the design but also the business operations and know how it should operate. If the logic of the code produced is not capable of examination by ordinary business people, we are in trouble. If the documentation of a system of processes cannot be easily examined, we are in more trouble. The results of continued modification of this code without respective changes in the documentation will be untenable and is the average condition in businesses all over the world today.

This book is for the above average business Executive who is going to lead his/her respective industry and sector to superior results. There is a better way and method and it is called *Model-Driven Development.*

I make no promises for any of the vendors who claim to be able to generate perfect executable code from logical models. Nor should your enterprise have to rely on such products or hype. What this book does is provide a gradual easily attainable path to efficient reliable enterprise information systems through better organization and the application of *Model-Driven Development* methodology.

Communication is the key to any software development. This is even more important for systems that lay horizontally across all or many of the departments within an enterprise. A formal program of first informing, then appointing a framework of leaders including their written mutually agreed upon responsibilities, and finally the adoption of a plan, strategy, and methodology is essential.

These enterprise systems are not dependent on any one vendor or developer nor should they be. They can be mixed and matched with what already exists including packages and contractor work that you have long since abandoned in trying to add on any more extensions. It is no 'magic bullet' and will require lots of pains-taking and consistent work to accomplish.

This book will also address the following topics:

- Data Quality
- Enterprise Central Model
- Enterprise Architecture
- ETL (Extract, Transform, & Load)
- Data Stewardship
- Data Governance
- BI (Business Information) Architecture
- MDM (Master Data Management)
- EII (Enterprise Information Integration)
- SOA (Service-Oriented Architecture)

3

PHASES

There are essentially 3 phases for any enterprise undertaking or project. The first phase **informs, educates, and trains**. The second phase **implements and builds** and the third phase essentially **reviews and evaluates** past mistakes with an eye to the future trends in technology and sustaining your 'program'.

The difference between an enterprise-level and department-level is scope. At the enterprise level all experimenting has been done. We are implementing proven designs with established tools and trained people. This is not for the faint of heart, this is not the time to isolate and do things at a low key so mistakes can be minimized and covered up. This is show-time and everything must be fully exposed and out in the open for everyone to see including the mistakes so everyone can quickly adjust.

If as Sponsor, Senior Executive, or Project Manager you feel unprepared, stop! Do not go any further, put this book down and go back and repeat the fundamentals producing better departmental or pilot projects until you are comfortable with your level of plans, tools, and personnel.

IMPLEMENTING ENTERPRISE DATA WAREHOUSING
A GUIDE FOR EXECUTIVES

There can be no going back once an enterprise-wide project is started. It is successful or no man comes back alive. Everyone is fired or resigns!

(Please feel free to make notes after each phase).

CHAPTER THREE PHASES

PHASE I - INFORMATION

Any large enterprise program must begin with a training and informational project. Think of similar programs that your company may have initiated in the past such as Y2K, EDI transactional sets, ISO 9000, Project Management, a new accounting package, BASEL I, BASEL II, HIPAA, or Sarbanes-Oxley. All are examples of enterprise-wide programs that ran horizontally across several departments and areas of your company. So too, this will affect all areas of your business that collect, process, and analyze enterprise data.

For most businesses, this will be the main general ledger data that produces the financial reporting needed by more than one department to manage and coordinate the activities of the enterprise. This will include the aggregated expenses and revenues from all lines-of-business. This must also include all the shared data such as customers and products that are necessary for each line-of-business as well as the dimensional codes that are so important in aggregating information. All reference data must be included. It is logical to centralize this data in order to better maintain it in the first place and it usually must be shared by several lines-of-business. Reference data is often called dimensional codes because they often are used to aggregate facts.

Phase I by necessity must start with a very aggressive and wide program of **Data Quality**.

People must first understand what we mean by data quality. They also must appreciate what is meant by collecting data in time and event chronology for later analysis. The online system may provide the answers necessary to process something immediately but may not make any sense 15 years from now if the context of that data item or value is not explicitly expressed or included with the data.

For example, if a stranger comes up to you and says, "the answer you seek is 123.19"; you have no idea of the significance of this number or how it affects you. It could be anything. But if he says, "your checking account at the First Bank has a balance of $123.19 at the close of yesterday's business", you understand perfectly what this information is and how it applies to your situation. With the proper context, the data is of immediate and obvious value.

Let me give you another example. Early in my career I was asked to support a regional accounting area that was responsible for making a number of adjusting entries for all the departments within its region which was the largest in the corporation. The cycle time for analyzing the monthly transactions was only a few days and the adjusting entries had to be made so the General Ledger could be closed. I had carefully architected a BI analysis area to maximize the time these accountants had to make their entries. I thought that I would do this by designing a set of predefined spreadsheets including the imbedded SQL to populate the vales that would provide the quantities necessary and their accounts for each type of adjusting transaction. To save report space on the spreadsheet I did not include the details of each aggregation. The first time I demonstrated this to the accountants, they were appalled and could not understand how I could even think that this is what they needed. I had eliminated all the detail for each aggregate (total) that gave them the context they needed to insure the quality of the data. They were so familiar with the detail data during the month that they were depending on their memories to validate the end of the month aggregates which they could easily verify with their many ledger lists. I had taken away the very essence with which they could do their jobs by simply showing the totals without the detail dates, accounts, department, and transaction quantities.

Without the proper definition including an explanation of how it has been collected and aggregated, businesses cannot analyze and "mine" their own data that is created with every business transaction. The BI person knows that every transaction represents a pattern of customer decisions that is invaluable to the business's success and survival in the wide market place of choices. In this example it is also useful to point out that account balances are usually not very useful in analysis. It is far more useful to have the inputs and outputs of an account. A balance represents a net of all flows usually on a monthly or some other arbitrary period that may or may not meet the analyst's requirements for observing trends over different or longer time periods.

Another problem is the dimensions of any data item. The analyst will often want to compare aggregates: departmental revenues or expenses, for example. Department or location codes are notorious for changing, merging, splitting off into different numbering schemas, etc. If one is comparing departmental revenues over 15 years without any comprehension of how those departments have been merged or split up or renumbered the results may be totally misleading. These are what the analyst calls **slowly changing dimensions** which may have to be adjusted to make meaningful comparisons. Auditors constantly look for these kinds of problems when evaluating Financial Statements so that stockholders of publicly traded enterprises are not misled as to the true nature or trend of revenues or expenses. The Data Architect must also be aware of these problems and adjust the data in a consistent and transparent way according to the rules that have been established by the business. This usually involves some transformations made when the data is loaded into the data warehouse structure.

Data is loaded, not closely integrated from system to system. This is what is meant by "loosely-coupled relational data structures". This technique is far more efficient and cheaper especially when integrating disparate technology platforms that are operating on different levels of granularity, i.e., monthly, not daily. It is what makes data warehousing so attractive for large enterprises. To the researcher, the data appears to be integrated from several systems when in actuality it is merely copied into a carefully architected and consistent structure which conforms to all logical business rules and relationships of the data for a particular subject-area analysis or corporate enterprise.

The following are some of the tasks and questions that should be addressed and the goals and deliverable for the first phase:

Data-Quality Training:

1. What is it?
2. Who is affected?
3. What needs to be documented?
4. How can we organize the effort?
5. What is included in Enterprise Data?

Goals/Deliverables:

1. Data Quality Program
Establish staff to teach and provide set of instruction materials, intra-publications to staff, and a focal point for vetting questions

2. Data Stewardship Program
This program must attract SME's (subject matter experts) to take on the responsibilities of determining what is included and not included in enterprise data and profile (define, rule, and document) all data within each subject area.

3. Central Enterprise Model
Determine enterprise subject areas and logical entities. Provide models abstract enough to allow Executives to make tactical decisions while complete enough for DBA's to create physical models.

4. Data Governance Council
In order for budgets to be shared and to prevent rippling effects of data loading tasks and activities and to separate political considerations from the builders, this council must be created.

CHAPTER FOUR PHASE I INFORMATION

1) Who is going to inform and train staff on data quality?

2) How will it be funded?

3) Who will be the main sponsor?

4) What will be the criteria to identify corporate data?

5) Will a Master Data Management program be initiated?

6) Who will start the Stewardship program?

7) How will the stewards be identified?

8) What will be their duties and responsibilities?

9) When will the data governance council begin operations?

10) What will be their roles & responsibilities?

CHAPTER FOUR PHASE I INFORMATION

5

PHASE I - DELIVERABLES

A. Data Quality
B. Data Stewardship
C. Central Data Model
D. Data Governance

Every deliverable in Phase I represents a body of research with lots of texts, vendor programs, and seminar material. All of these subjects are well documented. All are necessary and must be addressed and at least known to most of the actors before Phase I. This is just the logical place to declare them and fully implement them. The following are a few notes just to get the uninitiated started or to provide more definition:

A. Data Quality Program:
There are many vendor-supplied programs available on the market place. Larry English (larry.english@infoimpact.com) is the most prolific and he offers many texts, materials, seminars on the subject. Your main concern should be in the adoption of this program across a wide area within the Enterprise. Initially, people have to be informed and told that data quality is their responsibility and it is sanctioned and mandated by the Executive.

18

Separate programs may be necessary for Executive, Manager, Analyst, and Operations.

Cultures will vary by the amount of training required. Incentives are always necessary and the more the Executive gets involved and sets up a Data Quality Staff, the faster and more enthusiastically employees will accept the responsibilities of data quality and get on with the program. Generally, contracting with an outside group to initially organize, design training materials, and to present is not a bad idea. However, it must be done with the staff that will eventually take over the task. The problem is not in initially training and presenting, but in identifying the people needed to sustain the effort and also to identify the data stewards for the next program.

B. Data Stewardship Program:
This is the real lynch pin of the whole enterprise effort. Stewardship is not common in our society. It is a sense of personal responsibility for taking care of something that is not one's own and requires a high-level / low-level knowledge of a particular part of the business that often goes beyond the normal responsibility of this person's title within the organization.

The data steward must be experienced enough to recognize and understand the value of a particular subject area to the enterprise while at the same time possessive of and hands-on enough of all the data that goes through the processes under his direction and authority. These persons are usually identified by others and are often unlikely to 'volunteer'. Usually they are already too busy and have to be given incentives to participate in the subject area analysis, definition, documentation, and Data Governance. Their first tasks will be to organize the identification of enterprise data and profile all data within the processes under their control.

This is not as daunting a task as may first appear. There are many outside professional groups of meta-data standard bodies and regulatory bodies which can be of real help here. Our own Federal government, for example, has established several large meta-data dictionaries in what is known as "11179 Federal Registries." These registries can have real value here. Many of these groups distribute at very nominal cost a complete ontology including ISO, ANSI and other industry recognizable identifying element numbers. Some exploration here is in order and sponsoring professional groups is a very easy way to set up a support staff for your own staff for very little money. Or a consultant can be brought in to create a very informative study for the Data Stewards complete with meta-data repositories including international or national or industry definitions. Most Stewards when confronted with this material should recognize the value of conforming and mapping current data names and definitions to the more consistent terminology used by government and other standard bodies. This recognition and adoption is absolutely essential for the next program.

C. Central Data Model:

Many enterprises are not prepared for this effort at all. It usually requires retraining of any existing modelers and business analysts to work for the whole enterprise rather than one particular process area of the business. This is part of *Model-Driven Development* methodology applied to not one but all of the essential system processes.

Most analysts have never had the responsibility for abstracting an entire enterprise and are just not up to the task. The use of outside contractors and consultants is usually required. A logical data model must be constructed of no more than 60 tables that will be abstract enough to be useful for tactical decision-making. This group must initially work very closely with the Executive leadership to determine and define the Enterprise subject areas that will support all analysis. Consultants with particular experience in the client's industry may be very useful.

20

This group should also be very adept at creating very abstract models by hiding complexity and giving the Executive a fresh new look of the whole enterprise that is very useful for measuring the impacts of strategic as well as tactical decisions.

The Central Model will be supported by either one or two different data warehousing methodologies. Either it will unite many Kimball data-marts that have conformed dimensions and can qualify as a consistent analysis for all enterprise subject areas or it will be a CIF (Corporate Information Factory) model first introduced over 12 years ago by Bill Inmon, the "father" of data warehousing. Both approaches are very valid and very well researched, written about, and successfully used in several large enterprises. Both offer very complete model-driven methodologies which can be adapted to any culture. Here again, experienced consulting is well worth the money to provide a fast-track to success.

An ideal data modeling team is about 3 with a strong manager. The manager can be initially supported by a consultant but ideally the manager should be the best modeler. Such a team needs to work very closely with each SME or data steward in each line-of-business system. The interviewing process and creation of a corporate model is time-consuming and at first difficult to appreciate by very time-constrained production staffs. It is more important that this modeling staff report directly to the data governance counsel and provides weekly and monthly updates on its progress.

This staff should be able to create a sub-model of each line-of-business system within a person month of daily analysis sessions. An overall central model should be created within 90 person days of daily analysis. The efficiency of this group should be entirely dependent on the availability of data stewards or SME's from each business area.

It is also advisable to begin building the ETL staff at the same time. Initially, the data modeling manager can also supervise the ETL area to support the modelers in their source identification and data profiling. The all-important element definition, however, is always dependent on the Data Stewards and SME's. The data modelers also have the responsibility of discerning the business rules for each entity within their models. This must be done in close corroboration with the business staff. Use-cases are a very important documentation component here and should be completed as a verification of the model. The Data Stewards are the key to this type of documentation and verification and can provide significant input to many processes the technical staff may not even be aware of because they involve significant business process knowledge.

D. Data Governance:
Any enterprise program requires discipline for effective implementation. The amount of coordination is enormous and really requires some rules to prevent the effort from becoming a debating convention. A project manager cannot remain effective if he must debate every decision he makes with every stakeholder. His decisions must be carefully analyzed and considered by him before he makes them. But then, all questions of authority and budgets must be handed off to another group which can use existing Executives to provide additional coordination necessary when tasks must overlap department authorities and budgets.

By separating the political and budgetary dimensions from technical operational considerations, we prevent one usually very nasty obstacle. Too often, when a technologist can not get *his way* it is all too tempting to appeal to his political mentor or authority to prevent some activity that will cause too much inconvenient work. By separating the two very different areas, authority and expertise, the solution remains in the most logical area and does not involve technologists from making business decisions and business people from making technology decisions.

The composition of the Governance Council must include the Data Stewards who will provide reporting resources and process knowledge as well as all the Executives and / or managers who own the data sources necessary to support the data warehouse. Remember, the Project Manager has already submitted his Project Plan to the sponsors of this project. There can be no debate on **what** needs to be done only **how** it is going to be executed and supported. The Project Manager and his team have all they can contend with in deciding what should be done, when, and by what skill level. The Governance Council must contend with how the efforts will be funded when it overlaps several budgets and what is the most equitable way of distributing the costs, considering the benefits.

In many cases, there will be no benefits to the individual area incurring the costs serving the data team. Several imaginative methods have been devised to overcome this barrier including "framing" where a set of predetermined rules can be used to "guide" the governance council in very complicated (i.e., political) situations.

The Data Governance Institute (www.datagovernance.com) has carefully researched this topic and offers texts, training, and consulting in how to establish data governance in *your* culture. For example, some very imaginative solutions include creating a system of "chits" which can be traded among managers for future requests. Again, this is a very well known area which should be thoroughly studied and researched by a staff long before such an enterprise effort is considered. I recommend the reader to the *Data Governance Institute* for further study and analysis of this very important area.

IMPLEMENTING ENTERPRISE DATA WAREHOUSING
A GUIDE FOR EXECUTIVES

Several of my clients who were large bank and insurance companies have taken an inordinate amount of time in establishing a Data Governance Council. Very often, the need for such an animal is recognized but other more pressing issues always seem to get in the way. I have, therefore, often recommended that initially an outside consulting group be set up which initially trains and sets up the mandate for this group. This is not perfect science and the consultants can begin initially supervising the data quality program or responding to the data modeling effort by scheduling analysis sessions. The important point is to get the committee working and earning its credibility. It is too late to train this committee when we have a crisis in design or loading.

One more additional word may be in order on the staffing of these programs. By all means use consultants whenever appropriate to start, train, and present new concepts. But don't forget these programs have to be sustained over a 5-10 year period. The attrition levels of most large enterprises demand this kind of commitment but also the training of the present staff must continue.

Most Executives may need help in understanding the number of support staff required for Data Quality, Data Stewardship, and Data Governance. Again, there are many professional groups that one can turn to for very useful and practical information. Once this has been done, a little research in what enterprise programs have worked and failed in your particular enterprise may be in order.

I wish I could give more detailed guidelines of how many people are required for these 3 very important programs; but it really depends so much on the culture and the level of experience of the existing staff. One might begin with an inventory of skills and responsibilities that each position requires like Zachman suggests (see Bibliography) or simply do a human resources study with your particular HR department and an experienced

24

consultant. This would be a first good step and might reveal particular characteristics of the staff that can be utilized.

For example, if the staff consists of a lot of professional engineers, CFA (certified financial analysts, actuaries, auditors then data quality could be taught by their own professional or industrial groups. These principles and concepts of quality and governance are not only peculiar to computer science.

Some clients have been really quite imaginative in creating programs which provided very cheap incentives for participating in these programs. Before work coffee and donut sessions, bring your own lunch meetings, and after work awards and company sponsored family outings have all been employed to provide more recognition to those who qualify, accomplish, and lead data quality, data stewardship, and data governance council activities.

The point is to change a generation of values and attitudes. In the past, Data was valued only as a by-product and was not valued as a source of important analytical insight. Now Data is recognized as providing significant patterns of customer behavior and strategic needs in product or service investments.

IMPLEMENTING ENTERPRISE DATA WAREHOUSING
A GUIDE FOR EXECUTIVES

1) Have the Stewards completed all ontologies for every line-of-business?

2) Has the Central Data Model been completed and reviewed by the Governance Council and Stewards?

3) Have the Data Governance Council written and disseminated their Charter?

4) Will the Data Council be operational before Phase II?

5) Are there any projects that must be completed before Enterprise Data Warehousing can begin?

6) Have the Data Governance Council issued extensions to the existing Enterprise Model because of new strategic directions?

7) Have resources been added particularly to Operations to support the next Phase?

CHAPTER FIVE PHASE I – DELIVERABLES

_____

_____

_____

_____

_____

_____

_____

_____

_____

_____

_____

_____

_____

_____

_____

_____

_____

_____

_____

_____

_____

_____

_____

_____

_____

_____

_____

_____

_____

_____

6

PHASE II - IMPLEMENTATION

Now that everyone within the enterprise understands what is meant by data quality or at least to the extent it will affect their responsibilities. And we have working Data Stewards and a functioning Data Governance Council; we can devote our attentions to actually implementing or loading the data warehouse.

A brief word about organizing the ETL area is in order. This is a particular sensitive area especially when the fur begins to fly. It needs a manager capable of using all the tools and more importantly knowledgeable about how the tools should be used and staffed. A lot of preparation has to take place to initially profile, access, and test candidate elements. Someone has to supervise this or chaos will result.

The first requirement is to be able to understand the 'target' models. Former data modeling is excellent experience. The supervisor or team lead must be able to 'set up' valid 'source' objects. This will usually be many tables and their relationships. Usually it is necessary to set up staging areas where selected production sources can be loaded and transformed and sorted for fast loads. One supervisor is preferable to control all these activities. Please do not try to augment this with vendor personnel. Usually, vendors do not have the experience of knowing what it takes to staff their tools. Specialization here is important in order to create the efficiency required to support data 'pulls' day after day until the data warehouse is retired or purged.

Once the 'set ups' and 'targets' have been created and identified, ETL programmers can test and transform to their hearts delight, all vying for the fastest performance.

The next staff member to train is the documentation staff. Most tools now make it possible to record the last successful access including the embedded SQL used to access the data. All this has to be preserved for later backup / recovery and archive uses. There are lots of other uses for these people in organizing the incremental loads and matching to production schedules, etc.

Several operations or programs have to take place during this critical juncture. By now, all the careful analysis of the data sources has taken place and been made available on the most accessible data repository tools. Now a strategy for loading the data warehouse must be chosen. Please be careful, this is not the time to rush into a lot of ill-defined activity and to completely emasculate the operations staff of all its tools, people, and computer resources. Remember, this Phase can be done by a very small staff if properly organized with a manager, team-leads, ETL programmers (transformation), and documentation and schedule people. To this staff one should probably add an overall data quality person to test the results to make sure they conform to the business rules of the 'target' model and to validate the use-cases.

Like all tactical decisions we must first consult our central enterprise model. By now we should have several subject submodels which contain all the objects needed to support a particular subject area. There will be overlap of some objects between subject areas but this problem is handled by most modern data modeling tools. If there are less than 3 subject areas, management can consider loading the enterprise in one operation. Three or more dictate a mandatory iterative load strategy by subject area.

Using the central model, all the tools can be prepared with the corresponding meta-data and profile data for these targets and sources. All access testing can be recorded and all source elements can be tested for conformance to definitions and format limits and valid values. Much can be done to guarantee the success of the first scheduled pulls or iteration.

Load performance is always a problem. Sometimes, third-party software needs to be acquired that can turn off dynamic processes on servers to increase the performance against pre-read and validated sources. Other times, it may be a simple problem of procedure update such as requiring all SQL code be embedded within one JCL job, thus considerably lengthening the execution time to complete several JCL streams. Very often, especially in legacy environments, current operation procedures have not been adjusted for loading loosely-coupled relational data structures. Procedures have been designed for very conservative process principles which must be adhered to in moving processes from test to production. Data structures are not processes and are easily transformed in one step or "pull". The only code involved is the SQL query used to extract and transform it which can be easily tested off-line and within the confines of a PC simulated legacy environment, if necessary.

If one data set extraction fails, it will not interfere with other data sets in the same "pull". ETL procedures do not require the isolation that processes do in restoring an environment so a failed test can be repeated. Tools are helpful in providing SQL optimization, schedules for automatically executing "pulls" in a particular sequence with results reporting including all successful stats and errors. This can still result in errors and BI reporting against the final targets is always very useful to validate the final "target" data structures.

Practice makes perfect and this is why I like to set up the ETL area beginning with the central data modeling phase. This area needs to be created initially with one team-lead who continues to acquire staff and ultimately a manager. Initially, this area only confirms the definitions of the modelers and helps in the initial sourcing of the data. As time goes on, more can be expected of this group. Data profiling, collecting for the repository, transformations, initial testing of the performance of tools that will be stressed after the initial load strategy is decided, etc.

The data warehouse will definitely fail on the inability of the ETL staff. This can be an ideal training ground, if properly organized. Much damage can be done from this area so maturity and judgment must be sought after, appreciated and rewarded as much as technical tool experience.

IMPLEMENTING ENTERPRISE DATA WAREHOUSING
A GUIDE FOR EXECUTIVES

1) Are all the ETL staff members trained in their tools and organized?

2) Have all sources and targets been profiled and fully populated?

3) Has a Load Plan & Strategy been written and approved?

4) Does the Load Plan include a QA, backup / recovery, purge, and archive plans?

5) Has Operations been fully briefed on the load schedule and agreed to cycle times or server availability?

6) Have all security access requirements been fulfilled?

CHAPTER SIX PHASE II - IMPLEMENTATION

CHAPTER SIX PHASE II - IMPLEMENTATION

PHASE II - DELIVERABLES

> A. ETL Program
> B. Backup / Recovery
> C. Archive / Purging

A. ETL Program:

Extract, transform, and load refers to the loading process needed to copy data from existing message and transactional systems to the data structures within our central model or set of conformed data-marts which represent all the analysis areas necessary for our enterprise. If I can be forgiven for using a metaphor, it is the **kitchen** of our data warehouse restaurant. Presumably, all the information necessary for the customer identification, cuisine, and ambiance have been thoroughly researched and analyzed and now all that is necessary is to order the components and ingredients for the particular subject area (menu) that interests us.

Now all the cook does is mix and cook the necessary ingredients that conform with the menu according to a set of policies already agreed to that reflect the cuisine and customer ambience we are most interested in serving and present this wonderful dish in the correct format within our advertised wait times.

When the correct agreed upon data is loaded into the carefully defined meta-data model which physically, logically, and con-textually fit, then we have satisfied the searcher (customer) and he will return again and again to create the presentation that best represents his analysis and appetites.

A successful ETL program depends heavily on tools, but most importantly on organization and a trained staff. Certain compo-nents can be prepared in advance and organized for fast access. All the knowledge that can be gleaned from the Data Stewards should be put in an easily accessible and maintainable repository of data profiles. This includes not only data format, but very carefully written definitions which may include many data qual-ity prototypes such as how this item has been aggregated, its source(s), its common usage, synonym to international, industry, and regulated terms.

Some may question this but it is not uncommon that the ETL staff is expected to make some very quick decisions to find an alternative when a data set or source suddenly is not available and a substitute must be used or the load has to be canceled. Load times become very tight and are usually never cancelled once the data warehouse meets a certain level of maturity. The data values will simply be blanked out if no values are available or contain an error code that the person doing the query will un-derstand and know that some data is missing from his analysis.

Under these very stressful circumstances it is easy to under-stand how valuable some tools are that present the ETL programmer with a complete set of folders for every data item loaded that includes not only its format but its complete profile. This is so necessary when searching for an alternative. Some tools even provide a source and target folder so that there can be no ambiguity as to the identification, definition, and context of a particular element or data item. It should also contain the most recent copy of the SQL, JCL, and API used for its last successful access including a list of allowed values and a schedule of its next regular load time.

There are many tools on the market that can fulfill some or all of the above paragraph's functional description. Software houses such as Informatica, Ab Initio, Accenture, and SAS can do this just to name a few. All these tools are a matter of re-search, analysis, demonstration, and use within your enterprise. At this point, all the experimentation should be completed and a consensus achieved.

However, new tools are introduced everyday in this very com-petitive market and one must be prepared for the unexpected requirement or new software solution. Let your staff's knowl-edge and already well-established vendor relationships be your guide. Do not bet the pony on a brand new relationship from either your staff or vendor community!

B. Backup / Recovery:

It is not unusual for me to find a so-called production data-mart to not have a backup and recovery plan. Data warehouses can blossom into very large structures over a very short period. What starts out as an experiment soon develops wings of its own and now may occupy the employment of its own staff just to keep up with the incremental loads. Regardless of the type of load, some very basic estimates of the data warehouse size must be established so a plan for backup and recovery can be written and practiced. Fact tables are no different than other relational structures in that they are vulnerable to the same kinds of sudden power failures or spikes, disk failures, floods, etc. This must be addressed and procedures written and practiced so everyone will be cool and composed when the unthinkable happens.

It would be foolish indeed for a manager not to be prepared for backing out a bad load. The options supplied by vendors are many and varied according to your existing resources. Begin planning by inventorying all of the tables that support your data warehouse targets. Estimate how long it would take to backup and recover these tables and you have a fairly good idea of what it would cost if you lost your fact tables or operational data store.

In most cases, backing up the final staging structures that support your monthly load is not a problem. Backing up and sequencing the exact SQL used to ETL to your targets may be more difficult. If it becomes necessary to restore part of a fact table the SQL is just as important as the data. There are many tools built just for this problem.

It may also be faster and easier to backup your data warehouse by copying it to a SAN and let it create the backup. SAN's (Storage Area Networks) are designed for this sort of performance and should be used if available. A simpler strategy might be to backup all final sources from the staging area and re-create the data warehouse whether it be an ODS (Operational Data Store) or Fact table by re-loading the entire structure. An estimate should be made based on growth rates and sizes of these structures before choosing this course.

C. Archive / Purging:
An archive plan is also necessary and may mean the difference of whether or not a fact table or ODS can survive.

If the enterprise's business changes very rapidly and its products and services are also changing, there may not be a reason for retaining a lot of history for analysis. I am thinking of a client who had a billing data-mart which was loaded every hour. It was necessary to purge this star-schema every quarter because of its size and the limited benefits of further analysis.

42

Other data warehouses will want to purge regularly during every load to minimize the re-building of surrogate keys. There may be short-cuts that the analysts can supply that can be given to the operations people that will greatly improve their archive design. Whether purging is completed once a month, a quarter, or every load, the potential analysis will be affected. Sometimes the existence of a SAN can greatly simplify this problem because of their capacity to create backup tapes or near-disk devices that can restore certain data for infrequent requirements. The point is to have a plan which can be examined by several analysis areas to determine the best most practical solution.

IMPLEMENTING ENTERPRISE DATA WAREHOUSING
A GUIDE FOR EXECUTIVES

1) What are the performance metrics for the first iteration?

2) Can QA verify the content of the first load?

3) Can QA verify the efficacy of the key structures, purge criteria, and test the backup procedures?

4) Has the Governance Council reviewed the first load reports?

5) What load difficulties were encountered and were present
work-arounds adequate for the next iteration?

CHAPTER SEVEN PHASE II - DELIVERABLES

IMPLEMENTING ENTERPRISE DATA WAREHOUSING
A GUIDE FOR EXECUTIVES

PHASE III – BI, DATA MINING, AND REVIEW

Phase I and II are primarily devoted to designing and implementing the enterprise data structures. Phase III is where most of the benefits from analysis of these enterprise structures will occur. Once the data structures for your data warehouse are built and loaded then the real analysis effort can begin.

Does this mean that we can now completely forget our transaction and message processing systems? The answer is no, indeed! These business transaction systems are now loosely-coupled to the enterprise corporate reporting system. That provides management with some important options that did not exist before.

In fact, there have been companies who have adopted a full model-driven enterprise model for the express purpose of being able to isolate and quickly replace very competitive lines-of-business systems they wished to invest or divest. It is now possible to isolate those legacy systems that we have been wanting to replace with a package. Now instead of going through a very lengthy and arduous task of integrating our existing shared processes we can merely map the package to our Enterprise Data Model. Such an effort can be measured in days not months or years. We also have the perfect device to measure the impact of such a purchase will make on the enterprise as a whole. If the elements that must be mapped to the Enterprise Model are many, we can be sure that the effect will be extensive. If not, we can anticipate a much smaller investment in time and money to incorporate this new system. The central model also makes it easier to simplify existing process systems and to extend or modify them. By the way, if the new package being contemplated does not map very well to our central model, it is because it is not appropriate to our business. If our central model fulfills all the criteria of reporting that our management needs, then our business may not need packages that cannot support this reporting or who do not have equivalent data elements which are important or peculiar to our business.

The existence of an enterprise model of targets also makes it possible to produce more abstract models of the business that can be useful in all sorts of ways.

Figure 1 and Figure 2 are examples of such efforts. These models are also accurate. They have just hidden the complexities of an ERD (Entity Relationship Diagram) model

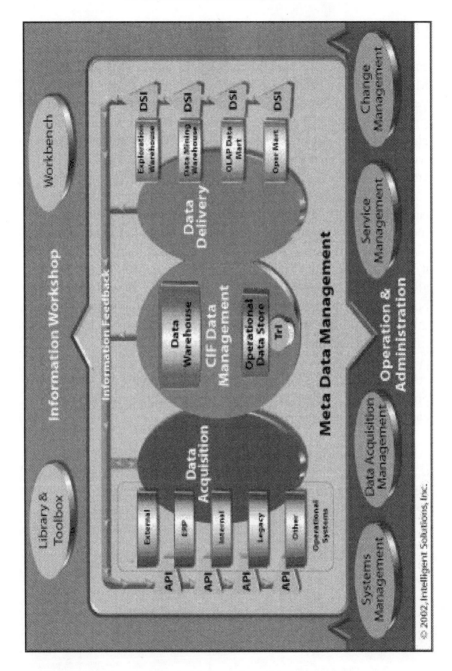

Figure 1 (2002, *Intelligent Solutions, Inc)*

that are underneath the ODS (Operational Data Store) and Atomic and Data Mart figures. Such attempts add greatly to the understanding and acceptance of these logical models. Too often, the business Executive is left with a feeling of bewilderment at the IT staff's attempts to explain the information systems that are supposed to logically reflect (model) the business.

This bewilderment can quickly turn to mistrust if the IT staff is determined to speak in techno babble and not offer to explain or extend their very technical diagram notations to include simple abstract diagrams.

Designing these diagrams also gives the IT staff better appreciation of the business and the important elements with which the Executive is most concerned. Further creative insight will often provide better communication examples for the entire company as well. It should also be mentioned that these diagrams provide excellent training materials.

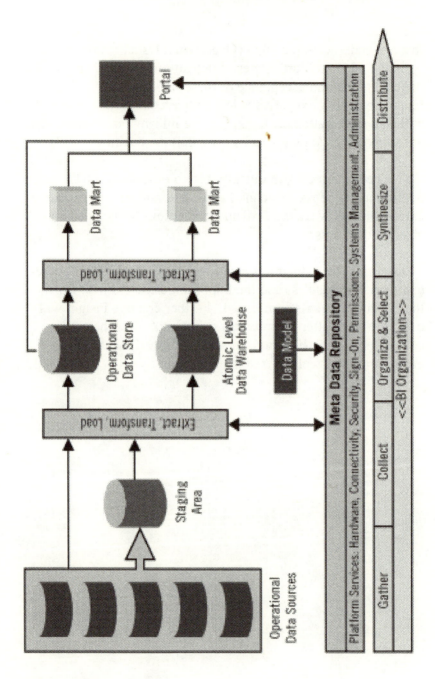

Figure 2 (2005, *TDWI*)

CHAPTER EIGHT PHASE III – BI, DATA MINING, AND REVIEW

Phase III will include the following:

A. BI Architecture
B. Data Mining
C. Master Data Management
D. SOA (Service-Oriented Architecture)
E. EII (Enterprise Information and Integration Tools)
F. Portals, Collaboration, & Other Content Sharing
G. Review & future trends

1) Can the affected analysis areas verify the content of the iteration load?

2) All the main areas need to be reviewed beginning with the efficacy of the Central Model, the ETL area and the BI-Architecture.

3) What lessons have been learned in the above areas?

4) Are there any subsequent projects that need to be initiated to correct or modify or extend the above areas?

5) When will the various analysis areas present their first results and what have we learned that affect the overall strategy of the enterprise?

CHAPTER EIGHT PHASE III – BI, DATA MINING, AND REVIEW

9

PHASE III - DELIVERABLES

A. BI Architecture
B. Data Mining
C. Master Data Mining
D. SOA Architecture
E. EII
F. Portals, Collaboration, & Other Content Sharing
G. Review & Future Trends

A. BI Architecture:
   Whether your data warehouse consists of a set of highly conformed data-marts or a complete CIF type of data model, either will provide all the enterprise data needed for Business Information analysis. Both will support a consistent meta-data that will be very useful for the BI / Analyst, his / her clients and the Executive management. The architecture will make it possible for very broad analysis both in time and across all significant enterprise entities.

   Regardless of the type of analysis, all will benefit from the standardized labels and definitions of data. At this point some

58

enterprises choose to model directly from the central model or import elements and build separate data-marts and report structures to better match the performance characteristics of their tools. There are all sorts of front-end tools available to match the particular analysis needs of each community.

For example, a community of CFA (certified financial analysts) may prefer a spread-sheet type of tool such as *Business Objects* and another community of engineers may prefer to use multi-dimensional cubes like Cognos. Others may prefer the report-like features of *Crystal*. All are valid and will interface with the data warehouse perfectly without any additional processes. These tools are capable of 'reading' the data directly and creating all sorts of analysis session structures through various point and click routines and scripting languages.

If the corporate model has been created with the idea of providing a consistent ontology across the corporation, now is the time to introduce new elements peculiar to individual areas of analysis.

For example, all accountants understand the need to express many of their cost and revenue totals other than the corporate monthly period when it comes to understanding customer buying behavior.

Perhaps, they are looking for longer term patterns at 5-year periods. Their analysis will tend to use different dimension periods that are not the same when comparing department to department corporate reporting. This is fine as long as we call these longer period totals by names that improve communication and not by names that confuse the meaning. Call it "5-Year Buying Period" and not "Customer Revenue." The BI-Architecture can add to the ontology but not contradict it for its particular analysis.

There will also be other changes that tend to be more precise and explicit than the general corporate meaning. Marketing wants to know very precisely when to record revenue. Too many commissions depend on this exactness. Something which is not very consistent will not please the general accountants who take a much different attitude preferring to generalize more and to make adjustments after the fact to make each period more comparable. This is what often leads to very confusing results. As long as each analysis area does not contradict the corporate definitions, more precise terms will add, not detract from individual department analysis efforts. Monthly revenues may be distinguished from commission revenues, i.e., mth-rev or adj-rev vs. commission-rev. Also, marketing cannot report monthly revenues that are unadjusted and compare them to previous adjusted monthly revenues.

Each analysis area must be carefully mandated to insure that common terms are used and that no analysis is done that will undermine the corporate meaning of common terms. The idea here is to logically add to our knowledge, not to confuse it.

There is so much more to be said for the BI-Architecture of each analysis community. The important idea to keep in focus is that they must all be consistent in their shared elements and definitions of those elements. Each BI-area should be encouraged to take on analysis that contributes to corporate enterprise knowledge.

Enterprises grow in fits and spurts, not smoothly. Individual areas tend to develop their own way of doing analysis and tend to call elements or objects that are useful by names that are meaningful at the time. Later reflection will recognize that these objects are common to other analysis communities and probably should be re-named. This is where the data stewards come in so handy especially if they meet in a council and talk to each other. Only such an organization has the capacity to routinely rationalize these differences in ontology and re-name these elements in profiles, documentation, and the corporate repository.

Standards cannot stop change, change must dictate new and better *standard* ways of how we name and define the elements that are important to a well-organized enterprise. One might even say this is the purpose of humanity. We live in a constantly changing environment which we make sense out of by carefully naming those elements that are most important to house the functionality we need. We constantly are building abstract structures to contain all the information needed to organize our efforts.

The individual analysis communities will also be sourcing their data for comparisons from many outside sources. Again, this is fine as long as we do not confuse the two and start reporting data that does not belong to the enterprise. Comparisons add to our knowledge but must be carefully separated and not commingled with enterprise costs and revenues.

B. Data-Mining:

Now that the enterprise data has all been collected under the guidelines of Kimball or Inmon methodology, management can be assured that their data has met the qualifications of "clean" analysis-ready data. Now the analyst can sit back and let the computer find patterns of customer behavior that are truly extraordinary and "out-of-the-box".

Affinity analysis is a good example of what is commonly known as "market basket" analysis. Here the computer samples all the values of a set of related data and produces statistical measurements of patterns. Usually, these "patterns" being examined refer to customer buying transactions or product buying patterns or whatever the enterprise finds interesting to investigate. Governments have used permit systems to indicate growth patterns of construction or even traffic patterns. Typical results for grocery store shoppers are like: "Men of child-bearing age buy beer and diapers on the weekend after pay day." Therefore, Mr. Retailer, don't put beer on sale with diapers or do place the diapers or beer closer together in the store.

Much can be learned about consumer behavior in this type of analysis. Many companies are making extremely good objective decisions based on Affinity Analysis. These kinds of data-mining efforts have never been possible before because of the large amounts of data required and the freedom to allow a process to access and examine all possible combinations to determine a previously statistically significant but, unknown pattern.

A word of caution, however, is needed. Affinity Analysis assumes that every data element being examined is free to conform to all logical values. If the data is constrained in any way which does not conform to the 'real' life being modeled, the statistical results may be invalid. For example, many health enterprises have a very important reason to be able to predict a causal effect with diagnosis codes. Health insurance companies would like to be able to say that they will not pay for any unnecessary test or test that does not conform to the science that predicts or confirms a particular medical diagnosis. This is a natural many-to-many occurring relationship. If the input form for the medical test does not contain all the lines necessary for a complete diagnosis, the results of an affinity analysis may not confirm the diagnosis. There also may be more than one ailment, there may be other tests that are included (panel of tests) only because the physician knows that the client's medical plan will not pay for certain tests if other tests are not also included or maybe the physician has no idea what is wrong and is just ordering a bunch of tests in hopes of finding something wrong on which he can base a form of treatment. The objective reasons for correlating diagnosis code with test code may be just too complex or may be a simple problem of not containing enough input lines. Statistics can tell us only what is significant about the patterns of data present, not data that is not present. Analysis expertise is still required to correctly interpret the results and insure that the data is collected properly and that it is not unnecessarily constrained.

Affinity Analysis is only one out of the six main areas of data mining that include:

- Classification
- Estimation
- Prediction
- Affinity grouping or association rules
- Clustering
- Description and visualization

All of these techniques have their place and are used for specific areas within the business to convey more information than the transaction quantities themselves. The first 3 are called 'directed' because they are 'directed' to a particular variable and the last 3 are called 'undirected' because they are used to establish some relationship among all the elements of a data model.

Classification can be very useful if you are examining all transactions, for example, to classify sales by product or customer type that can be detected with certain demographics association with the sale.

Estimation is particularly useful when examining records for customer credit worthiness or estimating household income. Some tools used in verticals are built-in to applications such as retail loans, etc.

Other prediction techniques use well-documented histories to match with transactions as a predictor of customer behavior.

The undirected techniques such as Affinity, Clustering, and other Visual techniques can be very useful in discovering new patterns of customer behavior. These are important for understanding new trends which do not conform to customer behavior history and can be very important for detecting new strategic opportunities that may be available to the business.

The real promise of data mining is to return the focus of businesses to serving customers and to providing efficient business processes without having the close contact of the buyer visiting the place of business. Our modern e-connected marketplace demands we develop more objective and less intrusive methods of understanding basic customer behavior. This will require more analytic knowledge and more skill to fully understand and discriminate when to employ a particular technique. Consulting is particularly important in this area. Staff participation in these activities is also paramount to eventually produce similar skills once a number of successful mining areas are discovered and exploited by the experts.

C. Master Data Management:
As so often happens in IT, simple expediency often gains sway over logic. In many IBM legacy shops, mergers and acquisitions have often created multiple versions of customers and products until the point that a new "master" class of data is required to bring uniqueness back to relational data bases.

It has also been my experience that a program of "master data" is often taken on in environments where meta-data concepts and 3rd Normal form has been a challenge. Regardless, half measures are sometimes necessary to clean up particular areas that are important to the enterprise.

It is regrettable that the entire organization can not be "cleaned" at once but a program of Master Data Management may be necessary before embarking on any enterprise program. Again, outside consulting is available and this may be the most logical choice for some cultures.

If your enterprise is proceeding on this course, fine. It may be necessary to 'clean' product and customer data areas before an enterprise project can be fully supported. Careful analysis should be done, however, for this effort may deter or considerably delay other areas from mining their 'clean' data. A subject area analysis may be important to isolate these areas and allow other areas within the business to proceed with advanced analysis techniques. Kimball has suggested this as a prerequisite even to departmental data-marts.

Master Data Management is a sub-class of the normal 'cleaning' of data and should not be considered as the only technique to employ on the path to quality data.
A good effort of corporate modeling should also meet the same results as an MDM program. Each culture will vary according to their needs for data quality. Some enterprises take well to a small group of modelers going around from line-of-business system SME to SME creating the ontology for each line-of-business and rationalizing that all into a central corporate model. Other cultures require much more aggressive methods with larger efforts to reform particular areas such as customer or product and then apply them to every area shared between systems.

Both approaches have their advantages and disadvantages. MDM is not a 'silver bullet' and must spawn other continuous rationalizing campaigns to produce a more consistent high quality of data.

D. SOA Architecture:
Service Oriented Architecture is a natural outgrowth of Model-Driven development and meta-data concepts. SOA requires that data be stored and presented with business context.

The basic premise of SOA assumes that architecture is essentially composed of highly modular processes which are highly reusable. SOA goes on to divide the world between services and consumers of those services complete with very explicit contracts. It promises to provide a discipline of rationalizing new processes similar to "normalization" that will be far more flexible, efficient, and cheaper to extend and maintain process code.

There are those who would say this architecture is long on principles and short on successful implementations. Regardless, it is consistent with Model-Driven Development and many OOA concepts that depend heavily on a complete and consistent repository of data element profiles, definitions, and documentation. This architecture is especially interesting from a conformance point of view and promises to reduce complexity as well as increase ROI of system development. Be sure that the Objects support SQL interfaces.

It is not necessary for an enterprise data warehouse undertaking, but can add considerable benefits to a successful deployment of an enterprise repository. Remember, you have already de-coupled the process areas from the central corporate model. This allows the individual process areas to be constantly re-worked for consistency and simplicity. Each process area is free to pursue efficiency by whatever means or technology without affecting the enterprise's corporate reporting needs.

E. EII (Enterprise Information & Integration):
Enterprise Information & Integration tools are totally useless in a data warehousing analysis effort. Data Warehouses are designed and built to measure trends in large amounts of data over long time periods. All data is read, never updated; only continually loaded each time period according to the planned granularity of the fact or ODS models. EII tools when combined with a BI tool can not only report but immediately update a transaction or message-based process that is the source of the reported data. This is unnecessary and fairly risky.

Analysis takes time to present and absorb. It is a manual process that aids the totally manual process of decision-making. The results of the decision process may change or add to the transaction process but should be introduced in the front-end of those processes and not the back-end. The confusion this could create with data out of sync is mind-numbing.

This is an interesting technical development but is not particularly helpful in an analysis area like data warehousing. I know this may be a disappointment to many readers but I don't think we are ready yet to turn the business over to the computer which will analyze and immediately correct business transaction results according to that analysis.

F. Portals, Collaboration, & Other Content Sharing:
It is very encouraging that so many companies now want to share their back-office systems with the public via the internet or intranet. Just like EII, however, a word of caution is necessary. Analysis can not be confused with process. A **portal** can either present results of previous analysis or provide input to a front-end transaction or message-based system. We do not, however, want to update the back-end of a previous business transaction just to see the results of a presentation available through a portal.

By all means, make star-schema decision tools available to the internet query, but do it in a way that allows the data to be staged and prepared for a limited Ad Hoc analysis area. Here is where segmenting data into logical subgroups based on years or whatever time group is logical will provide good access and even better performance.

The data structure and the type of analysis have to be carefully planned. This is why BI-architects may also create additional data structures even if the data is originating directly from a CIF atomic area. Not only is content important but also the logical context of the data. Sometimes, the architect will load from one structure to another loosely-coupled structure because of the flexibility it creates. This is fine and I have seen some wonderful agile reporting and analysis done in this fashion. As long as the additional structures aid in the continuous maintenance and understanding of the context of the meta-data and are consistent with the central model, then this approach is beneficial.

Collaboration of company-wide documents on an intranet is very cost-effective rather than mailing the same documents to every employee mailbox. Search capability is now much better using transformations to XML using meta-data standards such as METS (Metadata Encoding and Transmission Standard) and ALTO (Analyzed Layout and Text Object). Using XML documents can also be secured individually rather than by function, location, or password. This is a great boon to governments who may want to control classified documents through distributions that may present headers but not content. These are all very useful enterprise applications of data but have no place in data warehouses or BI architecture.

Other content sharing includes images which may provide real performance hurdles to the data warehouse. Various vendors have now made available compression techniques that make it possible to share images with analysis results. Many BI-tools allow this and to the extent that analysis is enhanced, images are encouraged. However, image libraries can be very space and performance hogs and should not be shared below the BI level. These libraries can be separate from the main Enterprise Model in a separate data structure that the BI tools can access just as they now have the capability of sharing various external public databases for comparison purposes and to incorporate in internal analysis comparisons.

G. Review & Future Trends:
A review should be conducted after the completion of each subject area iteration BI analysis. The tendency is to delay and put off these reviews until more is accomplished not wanting to ruffle feathers. Ignorance is the bane of any large enterprise undertaking. People must know their efforts are contributing to something larger than themselves to keep up their drive and mo-

tivation as well as to make immediate corrections to optimize the process.

Specific deliverables need to be re-examined. The first deliverable is the central model itself. What has been learned and what changes had to be incorporated into the model as a result of working with the data and SME's. There may be a pattern here that requires scheduling more interviews with different process knowledgeable people. This process must be repeated until the iteration results in no change to the central model.

Another area is the documentation produced for the ETL area. Tools can really pay for themselves in one iteration if they are properly setup and include all the profile and ontology (terms, definition, and relationship) metadata. Other data such as formats and access SQL are also invaluable. Some tools are capable of recording the batch program script (JCL) and SQL automatically for each successful access. This is invaluable and will pay for itself in saving valuable ETL-programmer time.

The last area that needs to be carefully re-examined is the initial BI-analysis results. It is sometimes forgotten by IT people that the purpose of the data warehouse is to provide better data accessibility for analysis. The business requirements for a particular subject analysis area have to be revisited and validated. Either the data warehouse structures have the right content or relationships or they have missed the mark. For obvious reasons, this step is often skipped but there are valuable lessons to be learned for other analysis areas that need to be brought to the surface even if there have been mistakes.

1) Have all loaded data structures in the Central Enterprise Model been verified?

2) The Central Model must be carefully tested mainly by the various analysis communities it was designed to support. Most BI areas will not be completed yet and will be completed in business priority and may include data-mart star-schema structures as well as outside imported data and other data used for comparisons. The use-cases for each BI area should be verified as soon as possible. Have all use-cases for each BI area been verified within the load iteration?

3) Have all load exceptions or design changes been analyzed?

4) Have all exceptions, changes, and possible extensions been reviewed by the Project Manager, Data Stewards, Data Governance Council, Executive Management?

5) Is it a complete success or has everyone on the Project resigned?

CHAPTER NINE PHASE III - DELIVERABLES

CLOSING REMARKS

This three-phase program when applied correctly and completely will produce remarkable change in any large enterprise. The future is quite clear when it comes to the importance of data accuracy, lineage, ontology, and audit ability. Regulatory requirements alone are reason enough, especially for public corporations, to adopt a new attitude when it comes to data quality.

The prerequisites of the first phase are absolutely essential. Programs of data quality, data stewardship, and data governance must be in place before the first phase can begin. For some organizations, this may take years. However, the risks are too high to proceed without them. Some practical benchmarks are in order. In an organization in excess of 10,000 employees with a central IT staff of 100 or more, the prerequisites of the first phase may take up to 4 years to establish. I have seen it take a year or less but even in a well organized company, it may take much longer. Don't be discouraged, it is still worth the effort. Some cultures are more used to large changes that affect all departments than others.

Remember, during this time a good well led and managed enterprise modeling group can complete the necessary interviews of line-of-business process systems and create a central enterprise model within 3-12 months. This work can be reviewed by an enterprise planning committee of Executives which should begin using this model as the basis for their more abstract models they can use in a number of varied tactical decision deployments and strategic planning.

Keep in mind the benefits and opportunities that await a successful completion of this program. Few organizations are in the position to make large amounts of quality data accessible to modern techniques of analytics, especially data-mining. It is now possible to discover patterns in your business transactions that may be the key to understanding your customer decisions, survivability, and industry dominance.

Objective quantifiable facts will greatly improve your company's ability to react and understand your products, market, and customers. Well-tooled, disciplined processes will also provide the flexibility and reaction time to greatly reduce your risks. Product programs designed to improve sales will be objectively verified by customer behavior in much shorter timeframes than traditional methods of conducting customer surveys.

It is also essential for each enterprise to produce their individual strategy for undertaking this program. For some clients, it was a matter of more objectively discovering the costs and profitability of a series of overlapping products and services.

Others wanted more clarity in the contracts that they provided for their customers. Still others were driven to this program by compliance and regulatory necessities.

Some clients had more imaginative strategies such as to decouple their processes so they could better simplify or replace them with better extensions or off-the-shelf software solutions. Some even wanted to get out of their present business and acquire or merge with other businesses.

Whatever the strategy, it has to be incorporated in the central model design. This may require more work especially if existing processes are slated to be replaced by new processes. This is where a disconnect between Executive and IT Staff often exists. Transparent communications are essential if better planning and analysis are to be achieved. Keeping everything confidential and then springing a large change on the enterprise never works well, especially for information systems.

The Executive needs to take courage and treat his / her staff with the respect it deserves. Even in the case of being acquired by another enterprise, the existing staff has much to contribute in the way of smoothly transitioning all systems. The presence of a central model will be invaluable and allow the entire management involved to make discerning and intelligent trade-offs.

After completing all phases, the program must be continued. New processes will be necessary because of new business. Old processes will have to be rationalized and constantly changed to reduce complexity. New terms, new objects will be necessary. This is not a 'dead' architecture but a living breathing organism that needs constant attention. In this way it will stay flexible and responsive to change. Given the tools that we have today there is no reason why even a large enterprise cannot remain flexible and responsive just as a much smaller enterprise. Our customers demand it and we might just as well plan for it before we become acquired by a more responsive organization.

GLOSSARY

AD HOC Analysis is the impromptu and flexible examination of data without predefined or fixed formats. Ad hoc analysis gives users the ability to ask and get answers to an infinite variety of questions quickly.

Affinity Grouping is a descriptive data mining task that describes which items go together based on a set of characteristics.

ALTO stores layout information and OCR recognized text of pages of any kind of printed documents like books, journals and newspapers. ALTO is a standardized XML format to store layout and content information. It is designed to be used as an extension schema to METS (Metadata Encoding and Transmission Standard), where METS provides metadata and structural information while ALTO contains content and physical information. This is a major contribution to text search performance. These standards make it possible to query as follows: *Find a figure with the title Ontology.*

Analysis Gap is a gap between the information that decision makers require and the mountains of data that businesses collect every day.

API is an application programming interface which is a source code interface that a computer system or program library provides to support requests for services to be made of it by a computer program. An API differs from an application binary interface in that it is specified in terms of a programming language that can be compiled when an application is built, rather than an explicit low level description of how data is laid out in memory.

Archive refers to a collection of records, and also refers to the location in which these records are kept. Archives are made up of records which have been created during the course of an individual or organization's life. In general an archive consists of records which have been selected for permanent or long-term preservation. Records, which may be in any media, are normally unpublished, unlike books and other publications. Archives may also be generated by large organizations such as corporations and governments. Archives are distinct from libraries insofar as archives hold records which are unique. Archives can be described as holding information "by-products" of activities, while libraries hold specifically authored information "products". Digital archives are now being used extensively by corporations to store parts of the Internet.

Backup/Recovery refers to making copies of data so that these additional copies may be used to *restore* the original after a data loss event. These additional copies are typically called "backups." Backups are useful primarily for two purposes: 1) to restore a computer to an operational state following a disaster (called disaster recovery) and 2) to restore small numbers of files after they have been accidentally deleted or corrupted.
Recovery refers to the method of restoring data after an incident.

There are various methods to accomplish a recovery depending on the hardware and software involved. A recovery can be a simple matter of repeating steps in a backup or loading script or it can be a highly sophisticated automatic process that restores several files simultaneously.

BASEL I refers to the 1988 Basel Accord, primarily focused on credit risk. Assets of banks were classified and grouped in five categories according to credit risk, carrying risk weights of zero (for example home country sovereign debt), ten, twenty, fifty, and up to one hundred percent (in this category has, as an example, most corporate debt). Banks with international presence are required to hold capital equal to 8 % of the risk-weighted assets.

BASEL II deals with the regulatory response to the first BASEL, giving regulators much improved 'tools' over those available to them under Basel I. It also provides a framework for dealing with all the other risks a bank may face, such as systemic risk, strategic risk, reputation risk, liquidity risk, and legal risk, which the accord combines under the title of residual risk.

BI Architecture. Business Intelligence Architecture is anything that regulates data transformation into actionable information to support decision-making to gain advantage in evolving business situations

BI Cycle. A performance management framework; an ongoing cycle by which companies set their goals, analyze their progress, gain insight, take action, measure their success, and start all over again.

BI (Business Intelligence) An approach to management that allows an organization to define what information is useful and relevant to its corporate decision making. Business intelligence is a multifaceted concept that empowers organizations to make better decisions faster, convert data into information, and use a rational approach to management.

BI Solution is a mechanism that brings together people, technology, and data to deliver valuable information to business users.

Clustering is a descriptive data mining task that divides data into small groups based on similarity without predefinition of the data groups.

Cube is a multidimensional data structure that represents the intersections of each unique combination of dimensions. At each intersection there is a cell that contains a data value.

Database is a collection of related data that is organized in a useful manner for easy retrieval. There are different applications of databases depending on the type of data to be stored and how the data is to be used.

DG (Data Governance) refers to the overall management of the availability, usability, integrity, and security of the data employed in an enterprise. A sound data governance program includes a governing body or council, a defined set of procedures, and a plan to execute those procedures.

DBA (Database Administrator) is a person who is responsible for the environmental aspects of a database. In general, these include: 1) Recoverability creating and testing backups. 2) Integrity helping to verify data integrity. 3) Security defining and/or implementing access controls to the data.
4) Availability ensuring maximum uptime.
5) Performance ensuring maximum performance given budgetary constraints.
6) Development and testing support helping programmers and engineers to efficiently utilize the database.

Data Quality refers to the quality of data. Data are of high quality "if they are fit for their intended uses in operations, decision making and planning" (J.M. Juran). Alternatively, the data are deemed of high quality if they correctly represent the real-world construct to which they refer. These two views can often be in disagreement, even about the same set of data used for the same purpose.

Data Mining is an automated process that uses a variety of analysis tools and statistical techniques to reveal actionable patterns and relationships in large, complex data sets.

Data Mart is a collection of data that is structured in a way to facilitate analysis. Data marts support the study of a single subject area, with all relevant data from all operational applications brought together into that data mart. Data marts may be of the relational (RDBMS) variety or the OLAP variety depending on the type of analysis to be performed.

Data Steward. In metadata, a data steward's role is assigned to a person that is responsible for maintaining a data element in a metadata registry. Data stewardship roles are common when organizations are attempting to exchange data precisely and consistently between computer systems and reuse data-related resources.

Data Warehouse is a repository for data. Many experts define the data warehouse as a centralized data store that feeds data into a series of subject specific data stores – called data marts. Others accept a broader definition of the data warehouse as a collection of integrated data marts.

Decision Tree is a model for breaking data into groups. A decision tree uses a statistical algorithm to split the set of data being mined into branches of a tree.

Dimension is a categorically consistent view of data. All members of a dimension belong together as a group.

Dirty Data is data that is uncleansed or invalid because it is missing, incorrect, or duplicated (redundant).

EDI (electronic data interchange) is a standard for the electronic exchange of business data.

EII (Enterprise, Information, Integration)
EII is the industry acronym for Enterprise Information Integration. It describes the process of using data abstraction to address the data access challenges associated with data heterogeneity and contextualization. EII tools are often used in integration to update duplicate files shared between online transaction systems.

Enterprise Architecture is the practice of applying a comprehensive and rigorous method for describing a current and/or future structure and behavior for an organization's processes, information systems, personnel and organizational sub-units, so that they align with the organization's core goals and strategic direction. Although often associated strictly with information technology, it relates more broadly to the practice of business optimization in that it addresses business architecture, performance management, organizational structure and process architecture as well.

Enterprise (Central) Model is a computational representation of the structure, activities, processes, information, resources, people, behavior, goals, and constraints of a business, government, or other enterprises. Thomas Naylor (Naylor, T. 1970) defines a model as ". . . an attempt to describe the interrelationships among a corporation's financial, marketing, and production activities in terms of a set of mathematical and logical relationships which are programmed into the computer". "These interrelationships should represent in detail all aspects of the firm including . . . the physical operations of the company, the accounting and financial practices followed, and the response to investment in key areas" (Gershefski, G. 1971: 44).

ERD (Enterprise Relationship Diagram) is a high-level data model-the schematic showing all the entities within the scope of integration and the direct relationship between those entities.

ERP (Enterprise Resource Planning) is a business management system that integrates all facets of the business, including planning, manufacturing, sales, and marketing. ERP systems are most often implemented using packaged software applications that support each facet of the business.

ETL (Extract, Transform, & Load) Processes which are responsible for transporting and integrating data from one or more source systems into one or more destination systems.

Fact table consists of the measurements, metrics or facts of a business process. It is located at the centre of a star schema, surrounded by dimension tables. Fact tables provide the additive values which act as independent variables by which dimensional attributes are analyzed. Fact tables are often defined by their *grain*. The grain of a fact table represents the most atomic level by which the facts may be defined. The grain of a SALES fact table might be stated as "Sales volume by Day by Product by Store." Each record in this fact table is therefore uniquely defined by a day, product and store. Other dimensions might be members of this fact table (such as location/region) but these add nothing to the uniqueness of the fact records. These "affiliate dimensions" allow for additional slices of the independent facts but generally provide insights at a higher level of aggregation (region is made up of many stores).

Flat File is a collection of records containing no data aggregates, nested repeated data items, or groups of data items, i.e., non-relational.

HIPAA (Health Insurance Portability and Accountability Act) was enacted by the U.S. Congress in 1996. Title I of HIPAA protects health insurance coverage for workers and their families when they change or lose their jobs. Title II of HIPAA, the Administrative Simplification (AS) provisions, requires the establishment of national standards for electronic health care transactions and national identifiers for providers, health insurance plans, and employers. The AS provisions also address the security and privacy of health data. The standards are meant to improve the efficiency and effectiveness of the nation's health care system by encouraging the widespread use of electronic data interchange (EDI) in the US health care system.

JCL (Job Control Language) is a scripting language used on IBM mainframe operating systems to instruct the Job Entry Subsystem (that is, JES2 or JES3) on how to run a batch program or start a subsystem.

MDM (Master Data Management) also known as Reference Data Management, is a discipline in (IT) that focuses on the management of reference or master data that is shared by several disparate IT systems and groups. MDM is required to enable consistent computing between diverse system architectures and business functions. Large companies often have IT systems that are used by diverse business functions (e.g., finance, sales, R&D, etc.) and span across multiple countries. These diverse systems usually need to share key data that is relevant to the parent company (e.g., products, customers, and suppliers). It is critical for the company to consistently use these shared data elements through various IT systems. MDM preserves the uniqueness of disparate technology platforms.

Methodology refers to more than a simple set of methods; rather it refers to the rationale and the philosophical assumptions that underlie a particular study. This is why scholarly literature often includes a section on the methodology of the researchers. This section does more than outline the researchers' methods (as in, "We conducted a survey of 50 people over a two-week period and subjected the results to statistical analysis", etc.); it might explain what the researchers' ontological or epistemological views are.

METS (The *Metadata Encoding and Transmission Standard*) schema is a standard for encoding descriptive, administrative, and structural metadata regarding objects within a digital library, expressed using the XML schema language of the World Wide Web Consortium. The standard is maintained in the *Network Development and MARC Standards Office* of the *Library of Congress*, and is being developed as an initiative of the *Digital Library Federation*. METS is an XML Schema designed for the purpose of: 1) Creating XML document instances that express the hierarchical structure of digital library objects. 2) Mention the names and locations of the files that comprise those objects. 3) Mention the associated metadata. METS can, therefore, be used as a tool for modeling real world objects, such as particular document types.

Model-Driven Development refers to a range of development approaches that are based on the use of software modeling as a primary form of expression. Sometimes models are constructed to a certain level of detail, and then code is written by hand in a separate step. Sometimes complete models are built including executable actions. Code can be generated from the models, ranging from system skeletons to complete, deployable products. With the introduction of the Unified Modeling Language (UML), MDD has become very popular today with a wide body of practitioners and supporting tools. More advanced types of MDD have expanded to permit industry standards which allow for consistent application and results. The continued evolution of MDD has added an increased focus on architecture and automation.

Multidimensional Analysis is a way of analyzing data in a top-down fashion by examining measures simultaneously broken out by multiple dimensions.

MOLAP (Multidimensional Online Analytical Processing) is an OLAP storage mode in which data is placed into special structures that are stored on a central server(s).

ODS According to Bill Inmon, an operational data store (ODS) is a subject-oriented, integrated, volatile, current-valued, detailed-only collection of data in support of an organization's need for up-to-the-second, operational, integrated, collective information. An operational data store is a database designed to integrate data from multiple sources to facilitate operations, analysis and reporting. Because the data originates from multiple sources, the integration often involves cleaning, redundancy resolution and business rule enforcement. An Atomic area is usually designed to contain low level or atomic (indivisible) data such as transactions and prices as opposed to aggregated or summarized data such as net contributions. Aggregated data is usually stored in the data warehouse in the ODS.

OLAP (On Line Analytical Processing) is an approach to quickly providing answers to analytical queries that are multidimensional in nature. OLAP is part of the broader category, business intelligence. The typical applications of OLAP are in business reporting for sales, marketing, management reporting, business process management (BPM), budgeting and forecasting, financial reporting and similar areas. The term OLAP was created as a slight modification of the traditional database term OLTP (On Line Transaction Processing).

OLTP (Online Transaction Processing) is a data processing system designed to record all the business transactions of an organization as they occur. OLTP systems are structured for the purposes of running the day-to-day raw data of business, which requires efficiency and minute processing of transactions at the lowest level of detail. An OLTP system processes a transaction, performs all the elements of the transaction in real time, and processes many transactions on a continuous basis. OLTP systems usually offer little or no analytical capabilities.

Ontology is a model of knowledge for a bounded region of interest (also known as a domain) expressed as concepts, relationships and rules about their properties and rules that govern how concepts participate in associations.

Ontology Models describe: what exists in a domain in terms of objects and events, how they relate to one another, how they are used inside and outside the boundary of the domain, and rules that govern their existence and behavior. Ontology is ultimately concerned with the consistency and accuracy of communication: Between organizations, misinterpretations in communications are addressed by ontologies that explain and reconcile terminology, jargon, and nomenclature specific to each party. Between systems, ontologies reconcile metadata standards, XML dialects, and database access mechanisms. Acting as a semantic translator, ontologies insulate each system from changes that might occur on each side of the interface.

Portal (Web Portal), are sites on the World Wide Web that typically provide personalized capabilities to their visitors. They are designed to use distributed applications, different numbers and types of middleware and hardware to provide services from a number of different sources. Portals are often used in conjunction with back-office systems to allow accessibility to customers through the Internet.

Predictive Data Mining produces a model for use with new data to forecast a value or predict a probable outcome based on patterns discovered in historical data.

Purging is a systematic method to eliminate those elements unnecessary for historical analysis in Fact tables of Star-Schema's and other data warehouse relational structures.

Relation is defined as a set of tuples that all have the same attributes. This is usually represented by a *table*, which is data organized in rows and columns. In a relational database, all of the data stored in a column should be in the same domain (i.e. data type). In the relational model, the tuples should not have any ordering. This means both that there should be no order to the tuples, and that the tuples should not impose an order of the attributes. Put differently, neither the rows nor the columns should have an order to them. Relational Databases have a very well-known and proven underlying mathematical theory, a simple one (the set theory) that makes possible automatic cost-based query optimization, schema generation from high-level models and many other features that are now vital for mission-critical Information Systems development and operations. In contrast, Object Databases will never reach these capabilities of Relational Databases. The Object paradigm is already proven for application design and development, but it may simply not be an adequate paradigm for the data store.

SAN (Storage Area Network) is architecture to attach remote computer storage devices such as disk array controllers, tape libraries and CD arrays to servers in such a way that to the operating system the devices appear as locally attached devices. Although cost and complexity is dropping, as of 2007, SAN's are still uncommon outside larger enterprises. SAN's are important to data warehousing as a backup tool for fact tables.

Slowly Changing Dimensions is a term that describes how dimensions reflect data changes over time. For example, business

88

locations, departments, product numbers are all used in forming comparable aggregates of revenues and expenses and slowly change over long periods of time leading to distortions if not consistently modified.

SME (Subject Matter Expert) is a person expert in a particular area. Invariably, the term is used when there are professionals with technical project knowledge but without expertise in the field of application. For example, in the development of complex computer systems (e.g. artificial intelligence, expert systems, control, simulation, or business software) an SME is a person who is knowledgeable about the domain being represented (but often not knowledgeable about the programming technology used to represent it in the system). The SME tells the software developers what needs to be done by the computer system, and how the SME intends to use it. The SME may interact directly with the system, possibly through a simplified interface, or may codify domain knowledge for use by knowledge engineers or ontologists. A SME is also involved in validating the resulting system.

SOA (Service-Oriented Architecture) describes an architecture that uses loosely coupled services to support the requirements of business processes and users. Resources on a network in an SOA environment are made available as independent services that can be accessed without knowledge of their underlying platform implementation. These concepts can be applied to business, software and other types of producer / consumer systems.

SQL (Structured Query Language) is a computer language used to create, retrieve, update and delete data from relational database management systems. SQL has been standardized by both ANSI and ISO. RDBMS vendors, however, all offer extensions to the normal SQL which often makes it difficult to use all the SQL code between relational databases of different vendors.

Scripting languages (commonly called scripting programming languages or script languages) are computer programming languages that are typically interpreted and can be typed directly from a keyboard. Thus, scripts are often distinguished from *programs,* because programs are converted permanently into binary executable files (i.e., zeros and ones) before they are run. Scripts remain in their original form and are interpreted command-by-command each time they are run. Scripts were created to shorten the traditional edit-compile-link-run process. Scripting languages can also be compiled, but because interpreters are simpler to write than compilers, they are interpreted more often than they are compiled.

Star Schema is the simplest data warehouse schema, consisting of a single fact table with a compound primary key, with one segment for each dimension and with additional columns of additive, numeric facts. The name star schema is derived from the fact that the schema diagram is shaped like a star. The star schema makes multi-dimensional database (MDDB) functionality possible using a traditional relational database. Because relational databases are the most common data management system in organizations today, implementing multi-dimensional views of data using a relational database is very appealing. Even if a specific MDDB solution is used, its sources likely are relational databases. Another reason for using star schema is its ease of understanding. Fact tables in star schema are mostly in third normal form (3NF), but dimensional tables are in de-normalized second normal form (2NF). If you want to normalize dimensional tables, they look like snowflakes (see snowflake schema) and the same problems of 3NF databases arise - you need complex queries which business users cannot easily understand. Although query performance may be improved by advanced DBMS technology and hardware, highly normalized tables make reporting difficult and applications complex.

Visualization is a graphical representation of data that some-times reveals patterns that are more apparent to the human eye.

Y2K The Year 2000 problem, the millennium bug, and the Y2K Bug was the result of a practice in early computer program design that caused some date-related processing to operate incorrectly for dates and times on and after January 2, 2000. It caused widespread concern that critical industries (such as electricity or finance) and government functions would cease operating at exactly midnight, January 1, 2000, and on other critical dates which were billed as "event horizons". This fear was fueled by the attendant press coverage and other media speculation, as well as corporate and government reports. People who understand how computers work recognized that finely tuned systems could get "confused" when the 97, 98, 99? Ascending numbering assumption suddenly became invalid. Companies and organizations world-wide checked and upgraded their computer systems. The preparation for Y2K thus had a significant effect on the computer industry. No significant computer failures occurred when the clocks rolled over into 2000. Debate continues on whether the absence of computer failures was the result of the preparation undertaken or whether the significance of the problem had been overstated.

XML (The Extensible Markup Language) is a general-purpose markup language. Its primary purpose is to facilitate the sharing of data across different information systems, particularly via the Internet. It is a simplified subset of the Standard Generalized Markup Language (SGML), and is designed to be relatively human-legible. By adding semantic constraints, application languages can be implemented in XML. These include XHTML, RSS, MathML, GraphML, Scalable Vector Graphics, MusicXML, and thousands of others. Moreover, XML is sometimes used as the specification language for such application languages. XML is recommended by the World Wide Consortium. It is a fee-free open standard. The W3C recommendation specifies both the lexical grammar, and the requirements for parsing. The only drawback for this language is its verboseness which requires as much as 40 x the original disk space. Some critics would argue, however, that the added disk space is immaterial because of the added benefits of portability and meta-data.

XML/A (Extensible Markup Language for Analysis) is a standard protocol that OLAP clients can use to talk to OLAP servers. XML/A is based on the widely adopted XML (Extensible Markup Language) standard and uses the programming language Multidimensional Expressions (MDX).

BIBLIOGRAPHY

Berry, Michael J.A. and Linoff, Gordon S., *Mastering Data Mining: The Art and Science of Customer Relationship Management,* New York: John Wiley & Sons, Inc., 2000.

Carroll, Lewis, *Alice's Adventure in Wonderland,* http://www.lewiscarroll.org/.

Carroll, Lewis, *Lewis Carroll's Symbolic Logic,* edited by William Warren Bartley III, New York: Clarkson N. Potter, Inc., 1977.

Coad, Peter, and Yourdan, Edward, *Objects-Oriented Analysis,* Englewood Cliffs, N.J.: Prentice-Hall, Inc., 1990.

Cook, Melissa A., *Building Enterprise Information Architectures, Reengineering Information Systems,* Upper Saddle, New Jersey: Prentice Hall, Inc., 1996.

Deming, William Edward, *It's All About Process,* MKS, Inc., 1995 – 2007.

Drucker, Peter F., *The Practice of Management,* New York: Harper, 1954.

English, Larry P., *Improving Data Warehouse and Business Information Quality,* New York: John Wiley & Sons, Inc., 1999.

FitzGerald, Neil, Byrne, Kelly, Coates, Bob, Edkins, James, Howell, Dan, Krinsky, Anthony, Liang, Eric, and Voloshko, Michael, *Special Edition Using Business Objects Crystal Reports XI,* Indianapolis, Indiana: QUE Publishing, 2006.

Hoberman, Steve, *Data Modeler's Workbench,* New York; John Wiley & Sons, Inc., 2002.

Inmon, W.H., *Building the Data Warehouse,* Boston, Mass: Technical Publishing Group, 1992.

Inmon, W.H., *Data Architecture, the Information Paradigm,* 2nd ED, Boston, Mass: Technical Publishing Group, 1992.

Jeffrey, C., *An Introduction to Plant Taxonomy,* Cambridge: Cambridge University Press, 1982.

Kimball, Ralph, *The Data Warehouse Toolkit,* New York: John Wiley & Sons, Inc., 1996.

Kimball, Ralph, Reeves, Laura, Ross, Margy, and Warren Thornthwaite, *The Data Warehouse Lifecycle Toolkit,* New York: John Wiley & Sons, Inc., 1998.

Marshall, Brian, *The Teradata database: Introduction and SQL,* Yucca Valley: Education in Parallel, 1997.

Martin, James, *Information Engineering,* Bk. I, *Introduction,* Englewood Cliffs, N.J.: Prentice-Hall, Inc., 1989.

BIBLIOGRAPHY

Martin, James, *Information Engineering,* Bk. II, Planning & Analysis, Englewood Cliffs, N.J.: Prentice-Hall, Inc., 1990.

McGovern, James, Ambler, Scott W., Stevens, Michael E., Linn, James, Sharan, Vikas, Jo, Elias K., *A Practical Guide to Enterprise Architecture,* Upper Saddle River, N.J.; Prentice-Hall, Inc., 2004.

Mundy, Joy and Thornthwaite, Warren with Kimball, Ralph, *The Microsoft Data Warehouse Toolkit With SQL Server 2005 and the Microsoft Business Intelligence Toolset,* New York: John Wiley & Sons, Inc., 2006.

Olah, Brian, *Impromptu Startup!* Upper Saddle River, N.J.: Prentice Hall, 2001.

Simsion, Graeme, *Data Modeling Essentials: Analysis, Design, and Innovation,* Boston, MA: International Thomson Computer Press, 1994.

Vitt, Elizabeth, Luckevic, Michael, Misner, Stacia, *Making Better Business Intelligence, Decisions, Faster,* Redmond, Washington: Microsoft Press, 2002.

Zachman, John A., "A Framework for Information Systems Architecture", IBM Systems Journal 26, No. 3, 1987.

IMPLEMENTING ENTERPRISE DATA WAREHOUSING
A GUIDE FOR EXECUTIVES

ABOUT THE AUTHOR

Alan Schlukbier is a senior data warehousing consultant with Schlukbier Consulting, Raleigh, North Carolina, (www.schlukbier.com or www.linkedin.com/in/alanschlukbier).

He is a frequent contributor to *Computing Canada, DMReview,* and other magazines in both the US and Canada.

With over 15 years specializing in systems integration, enterprise implementations of data warehousing, and enterprise data modeling.

He holds certifications in project management, management consulting, master data modeling, rational unified process, and joint application development.

Alan's education includes a BS in English, Math, and History as well as an MBA degree and is very active as a frequent speaker on enterprise software development, data modeling, and project management.

Alan's main avocations are meta-data, aviation, golf, and fly-fishing. He encourages your comments and is happy to answer any questions. He can be reached at: alan@schlukbier.com.